WHAT TAYLOR SAYS

THE UNOFFICIAL COLLECTION

WHAT

Taylor

SAYS

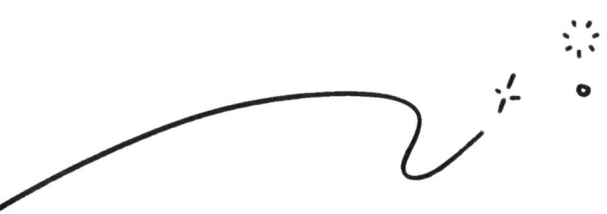

Quadrille

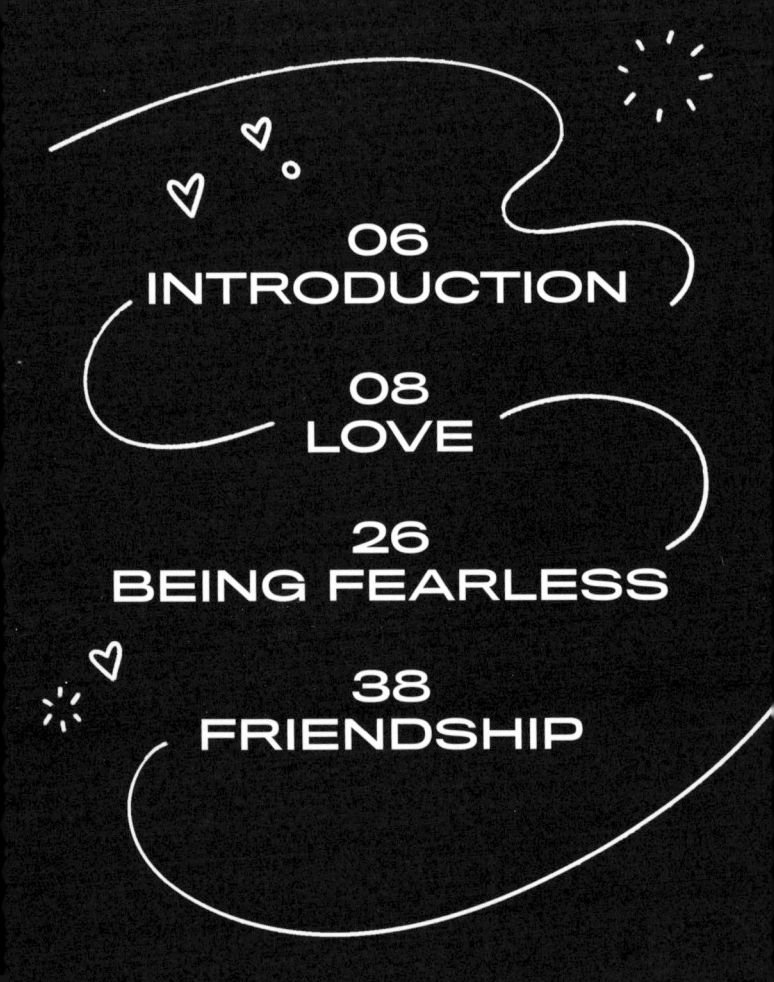

From hometown princess to global star, Taylor Swift is the world's favourite songwriter, popstar and all-round icon. Smashing records with her Eras Tour, Taylor has travelled the world performing her songs in front of adoring fans. She achieved incredible success at a young age, winning the Grammy for Album of the Year with her second record *Fearless*. Multi-million selling albums *Speak Now*, *Red* and *1989* followed. But the journey has not always been a smooth one.

A huge public backlash in 2016 left Taylor fearing for her career. However, by crafting albums that addressed her fall from grace in aching, heartbreaking detail, she gradually won over her critics. An epic run of music from 2020's surprise folkpop drop folklore, to the heart-rending balladry of *The Tortured Poets Department*, cemented her legendary status. As a renowned songwriter, she certainly has a way with words. The most famous blonde of the 21st century speaks with passion and incredible wisdom about her career ups and downs, and everything she's learned about life and love along the way, never losing sight of what makes her unique: her warmth and openness in both the best and worst of times.

"It's the most maddening, beautiful, magical, horrible, painful, wonderful, joyous thing in the world, <u>love</u>."

"You know how it is when you're going through heartbreak. A heartbroken person is unlike any other person. Their time moves at a completely different pace than ours."

"In a real relationship or friendship, you're shooting yourself in the foot if you don't tell the other person how you feel, and what could be done to fix it. No one is a mind reader."

"We're all hopeless romantics."

"It's magical if you ask anyone who has ever fallen in love— it's the greatest."

"I think that when people <u>fall in love</u>, it should <u>just</u> be about those (two) people."

"The worst part about a breakup sometimes, if one could choose a worst part, would possibly be if you get out of a relationship and you don't recognize yourself, because you changed a lot about yourself to make that person like you."

"My personal definition of beautiful is exhibiting an identity. I am so intrigued and drawn to people who know exactly who they are."

"All that glitters isn't gold, and first impressions actually aren't everything."

"I used to think that, you
know, you find the one
and it's happily ever after
and it's <u>never</u> a struggle
after that. And you have
a few experiences with
love and relationships
and you learn that that's
not the case <u>at all</u>."

"We are each a patchwork quilt of those who have loved us, those who have believed in our futures,

those who
showed us
empathy
and kindness
or told us
the truth
even when it
wasn't easy
to hear."

"I think the most profound relationship I've ever had has been with my fans."

"I've learnt that just because
someone is cute and wants to
date you, that's not a reason to
sacrifice your independence."

"[Love is] <u>tactical</u> at times, it's confusing at times. It's up to fate. It's magical."

"No matter what love throws at you, <u>you have to believe in it.</u> You have to believe in love stories and Prince Charmings and happily ever after."

"The only real risk is being too afraid to take a risk at all."

"In life you <u>can't</u> get
everything right. A lot
of times you make the
<u>wrong</u> call, make the
<u>wrong</u> decision. Say
the <u>wrong</u> thing."

"Grow a backbone, trust your (gut,) and know when to strike back."

"I'm always going to care. There's never going to be a time where I'm going to be nonchalant or casual."

"A lot of the best things I ever did creatively were things that I had to really fight—and I mean aggressively fight—to have happen."

"There might be times
when you put your whole
heart and soul into something,
and it is met with cynicism
or scepticism, but you
can't let that crush you."

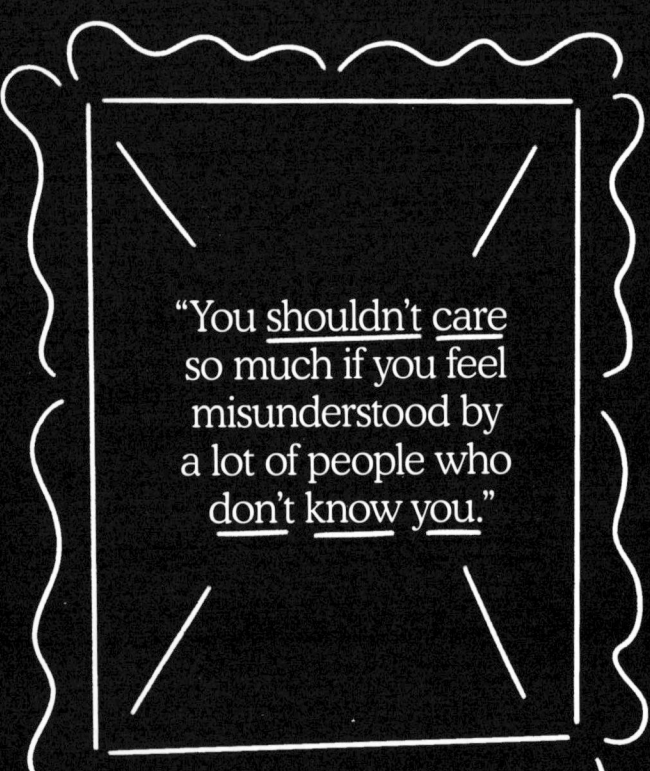

"You <u>shouldn't</u> <u>care</u> so much if you feel misunderstood by a lot of people who <u>don't</u> <u>know</u> <u>you</u>."

"Trying
and failing
and trying
again and
failing again
is normal."

"Life is short. Have adventures."

"<u>Never</u> be ashamed of trying.
Effortlessness is a myth."

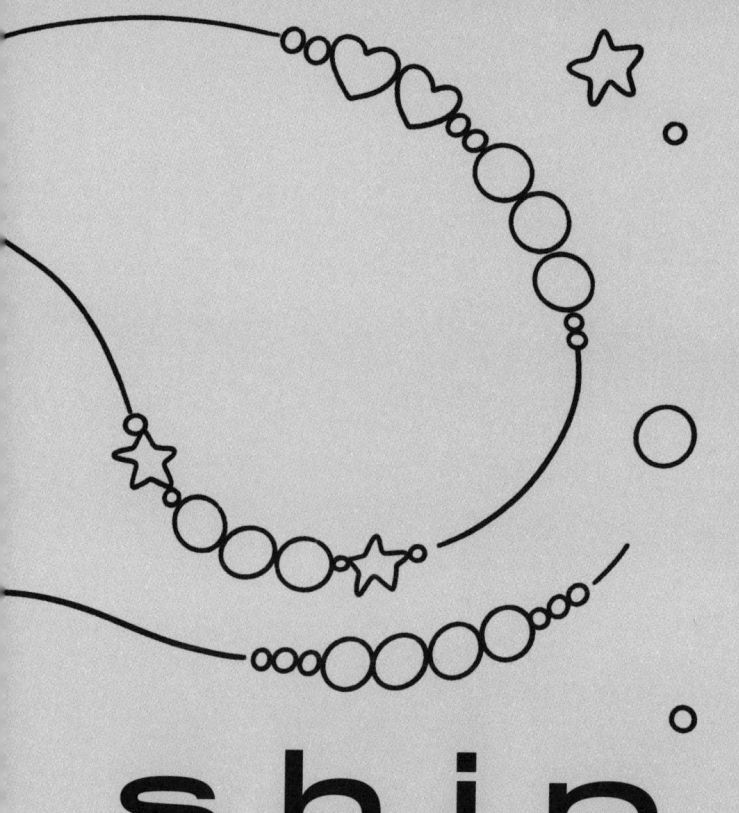

ship

"I surround myself with smart, beautiful, passionate, driven, ambitious women. Other women who are killing it should motivate you, thrill you, challenge you and inspire you."

"Loyalty is probably the most important character trait."

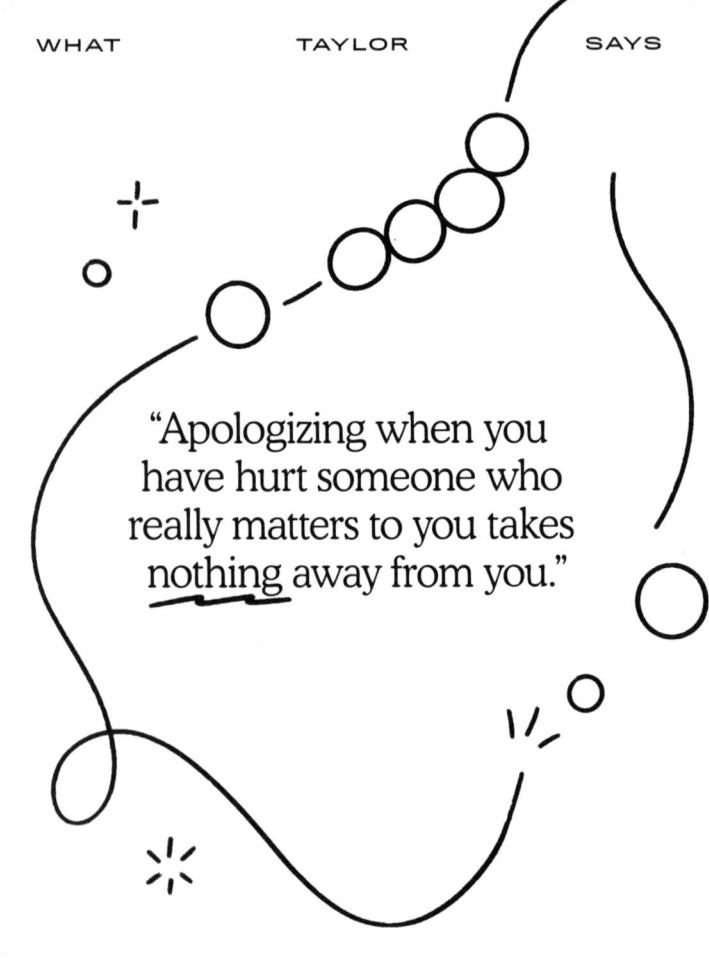

"Apologizing when you have hurt someone who really matters to you takes nothing away from you."

"Never being
popular as
a kid was
always an
insecurity
for me."

"I'm pleasantly surprised by the fact that I tell my friends absolutely <u>everything</u> and it never ends up getting out."

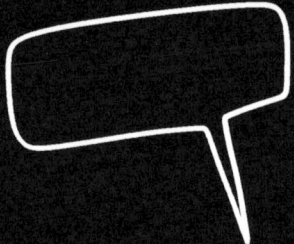

"I do <u>not</u> give an edited version of myself to my friends."

"My girlfriends and I talk
a lot about feminism and
the inequality between
the way men and women
are talked about."

"You only have so much room in your life and so much energy to give to those in it. Be discerning."

"You have to kind of give people the space to learn lessons in their own time."

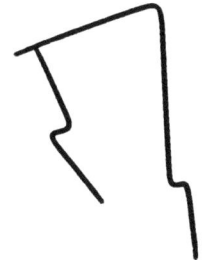

"My mistakes are very loud. When I make a mistake, it echoes through the canyons of the world."

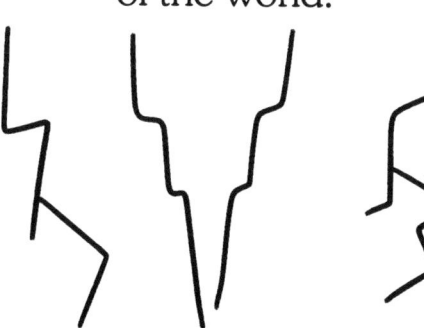

"I equate my 20s to walking into a costume shop and trying on all these different costumes."

"I wanna love glitter and also stand up for the double standards that exist in our society. I wanna <u>wear</u> <u>pink</u> and tell you how I feel about <u>politics</u> and I <u>don't</u> think that those things have to cancel each other out."

"I'm a woman, not a coat hanger. I need to feel healthy in my life and I need to take pleasure in food."

"Enthusiasm can protect you from <u>anything</u>. You can come back, even if you have a failure, you're rejected or criticised for something, you can become enthusiastic about the <u>next</u> <u>thing</u>."

"You can't
micromanage life,
it turns out."

"I'm sick of <u>women</u> not being able to say that they <u>have</u> <u>strategic</u> <u>business</u> <u>minds</u>—because male artists are allowed to. And so I'm <u>sick</u> and <u>tired</u> of having to pretend like I don't mastermind my own business."

"It's only a <u>flaw</u> when you make p<u>eople-pleasin</u>g a part of your personality so much so that you don't really know what is your opinion."

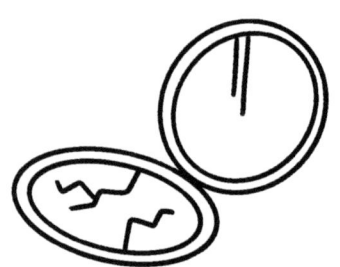

"I've been given a tiara, then had it taken away."

"I don't like to scream at the audience, I like to talk to them."

"I was always such a
<u>planner</u> and such a <u>list
maker</u> and lists of dreams
and goals and things I
wanted to do. And I think
my <u>new</u> list will be like
places I want to see in
the world, adventures I
want to have, experiences
I want to have, things
I want to learn."

"I need my tour to be _better_ than my last tour. I need my album to be _better_ than my last album."

"Just because something's <u>cliche</u> doesn't mean that it's not something that's <u>awesome</u>."

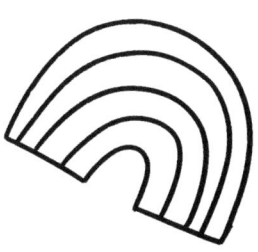

"I've always written all my own music. I've always made all of my own decisions. I've always curated absolutely everything."

"I can live my life <u>without</u> any public approval and (still) have a really really <u>wonderful</u> life."

The greatest

"Coming from <u>Nashville</u> there's always going to be an element of <u>storytelling</u> in what I do."

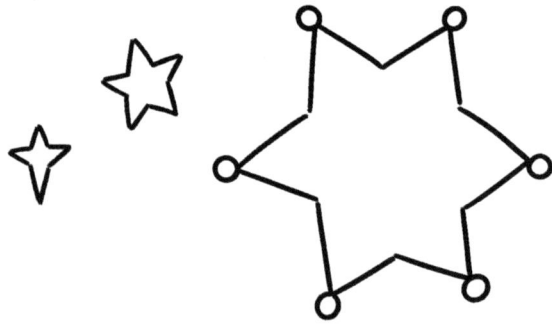

"I started writing songs when I was 12 and since then, it's been the compass guiding my life, and in turn, my life guided my writing."

"<u>Music</u> is the only thing that's ever fit me like that little black dress you wear <u>every</u> <u>single</u> <u>time</u> you go out."

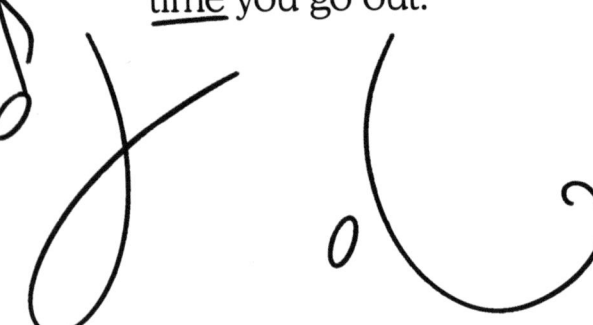

"I have
to write
100 songs
before
you write
the first
good one."

"Journaling was what made me discover that I loved poetry and poetry is so close to songwriting. If you start to write in your free time and make writing something that you look forward to, who knows where it will take you?"

"Have a <u>sharp pen</u>, and a thin skin, and an <u>open heart</u>."

"You never know how you're going to get an idea because it never happens the same way twice."

"Being a songwriter means you're very attuned to your own intuition and your own feelings even if they hurt."

"It can get complicated on every other level, but the songwriting is still the same uncomplicated process it was when I was 12 years old writing songs in my room."

"I've had several <u>upheavals</u> in my career. When I was 18, they were like, "She doesn't really write those songs." So my third album I wrote by myself as a reaction to that."

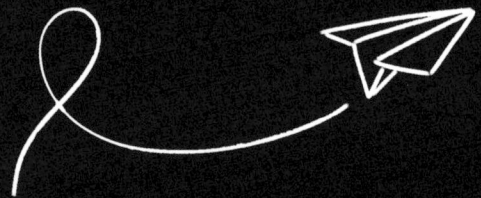

"Everybody in music has their own <u>niche</u> specialty thing that they do that sets them apart from everybody else, and my storytelling is what it is for me."

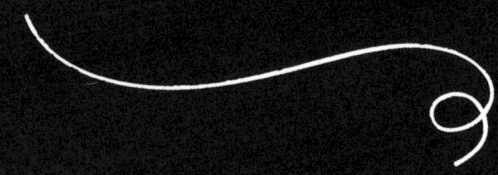

"My response to anything that happens, good or bad, is to keep making things. Keep making art."

"Some songs and albums represent <u>seasons</u> of our lives, like relationships that we hold dear in our memories but had their time and place in the past."

"I definitely feel more <u>free</u> to create now. And I'm making more albums at a more rapid pace than I ever did before, because I think the more art you create, hopefully the less <u>pressure</u> you put on yourself."

Coming back

"Getting <u>canceled</u> on the internet and nearly <u>losing</u> my career gave me an excellent knowledge of <u>all</u> the types of wine."

"All these things taught me something that I never could have learned in a way that didn't hurt as much."

"Every part of you that you've ever been, every <u>phase</u> you've ever gone through, was you working it out in that moment with the information you had available to you at the time."

"I respond to extreme pain with defiance."

"Criticism that's <u>constructive</u> is helpful to my character growth. Baseless criticism is stuff I've got to toss out now."

"Decide what is yours to hold and let the rest go. Oftentimes the good things in your life are lighter anyway, so there's more room for them."

"My experience has been that my **mistakes** led to the **best** things in my life."

"Hard things will happen to us. We will recover. We will learn from it. We will grow more resilient because of it."

"I needed a new <u>challenge</u> and there's no bigger challenge than uprooting your life, finding new places to hang out, new friendship circles..."

"With every reinvention, I never wanted to tear down my house. 'Cause <u>I built this house."</u>

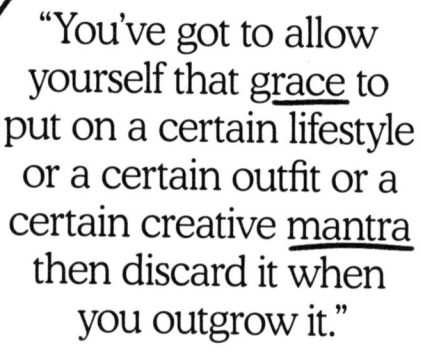

"You've got to allow yourself that <u>grace</u> to put on a certain lifestyle or a certain outfit or a certain creative <u>mantra</u> then discard it when you outgrow it."

"My hope for the future, not just in the music industry, but in every young girl I meet…is that they all realize their worth and ask for it."

SOURCES

Apple Music,
16th December 2020
– pp. **24, 41, 48, 59, 92**

BBC Radio 1,
13th September 2019
– pp. **61, 62, 63**

BBC Radio 1,
11th November 2014
– pp. **53, 66**

British Vogue,
5th December 2019
– pp. **50, 52, 56**

Camels & Chocolate,
27th October 2014 – p. **17**

Cosmopolitan,
31st October 2014
– pp. **23, 46, 90**

Elle,
7th May 2015
– pp. **11, 14**

Elle,
6th March 2019
– pp. **12, 18, 30,
35, 42, 43**

Esquire,
7th July 2023 – p. **68**

ExtraTV,
30th April 2015 – p. **60**

Fearless Album Liner Notes,
2008 – p. **25**

Harper's Bazaar,
10th July 2018 – p. **74**

Miss Americana,
Netflix, 2020 – pp. **51, 71, 76**

NPR, 31st October 2014
– p. **19**

On stage at NYU's Spring 2022
Graduation Ceremony,
18th May 2022
– pp. **20–21, 37, 47, 67,
82, 87, 88, 89**

On stage at the BRIT Awards,
11th May 2021 – p. **33**

On stage in Glendale,
Arizona for the Reputation
Stadium Tour,
8th May 2018 – p. **34**

Rolling Stone,
18th September 2019
– pp. **29, 32, 55, 75, 86**

Scholastic Web Chat,
29th October 2014
– pp. **70, 72**

The Guardian,
24th August 2019
– p. **54**

The Hollywood Reporter,
17th October 2012
– pp. **15, 16**

The New York Times,
20th October 2010 – p. **31**

The New Yorker,
3rd October 2011 – p. **13**

The Wall Street Journal,
7th July 2014
– pp. **28, 78, 93**

Time,
13th November 2014
– pp. **40, 58, 73**

Time,
6th December 2023
– pp. **36, 57, 77, 84, 85**

Vanity Fair,
15th March 2013 – p. **69**

Vanity Fair,
11th August 2015 – p. **45**

Variety,
12th December 2022 – p. **79**

Vogue,
24th January 2012 – p. **10**

Vogue,
19th April 2016 – p. **44**

Vogue,
8th August 2019
– pp. **49, 83, 91**

Yahoo Entertainment,
6th November 2014
– p. **22**

Quadrille, Penguin Random House UK, One Embassy Gardens, 8 Viaduct Gardens, London SW11 7BW

Quadrille Publishing Limited is part of the Penguin Random House group of companies whose addresses can be found at global. penguinrandomhouse.com

Penguin Random House UK

Published by Quadrille in 2025

www.penguin.co.uk

A CIP catalogue record for this book is available from the British Library

ISBN 978-1-83783-385-6

10 9 8 7 6 5 4 3 2 1

Publishing Director: Kajal Mistry
Senior Commissioning Editor: Kate Burkett
Editorial Assistant: Harriet Thornley
Design and Illustration: Double Slice Studio (Amelia Leuzzi and Bonnie Eichelberger)
Production Controller: Sumayyah Waheed

Colour reproduction by p2d

Printed in China by RR Donnelley Asia

Printing Solution Limited

The authorised representative in the EEA is Penguin Random House Ireland, Morrison Chambers, 32 Nassau Street, Dublin D02 YH68.

Penguin Random House is committed to a sustainable future for our business, our readers and our planet. This book is made from Forest Stewardship Council® certified paper.